THE BONHOEFFER CHRISM MASS

INVOKED BY THE MARTYRDOM OF DIETRICH BONHOEFFER

and published in commemoration of its seventy-fifth anniversary

Christopher D. Rodkey

The Bonhoeffer Chrism Mass

invoked by the martyrdom of

Dietrich Bonhoeffer

and published in commemoration of its seventy-fifth anniversary

Second edition

Christopher D. Rodkey

Barber's Son Press

York, Pennsylvania

Published by

BARBER'S SON PRESS

York, Pennsylvania

© 2020 Christopher Demuth Rodkey. Reflections © The Authors. All rights reserved.

Library of Congress Control Number: 2020931264.

ISBN: 978-1-7347188-0-5.

Barber's Son Press Publication #2.

Second Edition.

10   9   8   7   6   5   4   3   2   1

TABLE OF CONTENTS

Preface: Implication *iii*

Introduction to the Chrism Mass 1

The Chrism Mass 9

Reflections 31

    A Disciple's Prayer 33
       John Bair

    on a cross like a body on a tree 36
       Carla Christopher

    When I Remember Bonhoeffer, 37
    I Feel Like a Fool
       John B. Cobb, Jr.

    God Calls, God Bids Us Come and Die 38
       John C. Dorhauer

    Losing May Be the Only Win Possible 39
       Jon Ivan Gill

    God Did Not Choose 40
       Jeff Hood

    Pushed out of the World 42
       Josh de Keijzer

We May End up at the Gallows 45
　　Kristina Lizardy-Hajbi

What Will Lead Us out onto the Street? 46
　　Jordan E. Miller

The Patron Saint of Preachers Who Suck 47
　　Christopher D. Rodkey

Appendices

I. Suggested Readings for the Chrism Mass 51

II. A Bonhoeffer Calendarium 59

III. A Bonhoeffer Conspectus 69

Author and Contributors 71

PREFACE

IMPLICATION

I was surprised to not find any materials or commemorative guides to recognize the semisesquicentennial, that is, the seventy-fifth anniversary, of the martyrdom of Dietrich Bonhoeffer, *especially* given that this day (April 9, 2020) is also Maundy Thursday on the western liturgical calendar. This little book is a result of this observation, believing that *we*—as in those of us who remain in the church—ought to turn to Bonhoeffer regularly.

Not only is Bonhoeffer one of the most important theological thinkers of the past century, his writings have opened the door for an enormous amount of creative religious thinking which help us to understand the current world in which we live after the death of Christendom. Bonhoeffer understood that our post-Christendom era had already commenced, but we can look back to his stunning, later writings as one among many martyrs and one among many twentieth-century letters from prisons; one among too few Christians willing to stand up against Christendom when it is manifested in its most evil forms.

Here is not the place to review Bonhoeffer's life or to explain in detail his importance or legacy. However, I will not pretend that this project is divorced from the contrary and divergent interpretations of Bonhoeffer's life and writings. Bonhoeffer's recent, early twenty-first century influence among nationalist American evangelicalism is well documented, unfortunate, and a consequence of the very same evil that led to his execution. The church throughout history has always combated faithful existential and theological threats within itself by assimilating them into the inherent system of Christian thought and practice in one way or another—usually by castrating their true theological innovation. Examples of this include the threats of monasticism, medieval mystical writing by women, and the prevalence of Dante's *Divine Comedy* in popular Christian belief. In like manner the Bonhoeffer known by most American Christians today is branded and claimed by neo-Confederate religious partisans as a strong example of the White Savior who stands against whatever their movement feels to be undeniably wrong.

This popular Bonhoeffer, though, is a symbolic and "strong" Bonhoeffer; whereas the Bonhoeffer who actually lived was a real, humble person: a real pastor, a real son, a real lover, a real martyr. He was a theologian who lived on boundaries which shifted and morphed the limits of human morality and human evil. The Bonhoeffer who actually existed lived with the weakness of God (1 Corinthians 1:25) and the self-negating outpouring of Christ (Philippians 2:7). He wrote:

> Thus our coming of age leads us to a truer recognition of our situation before God. God would have us know that we must live as those who manage their lives without God. The same God who is with us is the God who forsakes us (Mark 15:34!). The same God who makes us to live in the world without the working hypothesis of God is the God before whom we stand continually. Before God, and with God, we live without God. God consents to be pushed out of the world and onto the cross; God is weak and powerless in the world and in precisely this way, and only so, is at our side and helps us. Matt 8:17 makes it quite clear that Christ help us not by virtue of his omnipotence but

rather by virtue of his weakness and suffering! ....
To this extent, one may say that the previously
described development toward the world's coming
of age, which has cleared the way by eliminating a
false notion of God, frees us to see the God of the
Bible, who gains ground and power in the world by
being powerless.[1]

While Bonhoeffer's writings at the end of his life challenge
every aspect of the "strong" and popular American
Bonhoeffer, those radical writings should be understood
within the context of his larger body of writing along with
his biography.

His most challenging writings neither cancel nor
supersede the rest of what we know about the early
Bonhoeffer. Rather, they are an extension and consequence
of a complex individual who remained faithful to the
church the more it betrayed him; a seasoned pastor whose
involvement with the ecumenical movement and work as a
youth pastor are often ignored; and a sophisticated thinker
whose ideas encompass and challenge the theology of
Barth and the philosophy of Schelling. His inspiration
from the witness of African-American Christianity should
not be ignored. Bonhoeffer's apparent ecclesiastical
orthodoxies are as complicated as his apparent ideological
heterodoxy; he does not fit squarely into a single label or
category. Yet we should always point out that his
heterodoxy was understood by him as a commitment to
orthodoxy, and that his understanding of orthodoxy was,
at the end, knowingly and blatantly heterodox.

He was, in the view of Empire, a terrorist.

---

[1] Dietrich Bonhoeffer, *Letters and Papers from Prison* (16. July 1944),
DBWE 478-480, in *The Bonhoeffer Reader*, ed. C. Green and M.
DeJonge (Minneapolis, Fortress, 2013), 802-803.

Yet in essence, Bonhoeffer was a *pastor*, committing heresy for the sake of Christ. I believe this to be his greatest legacy. As pastor, he was committed to the liturgical and intellectual histories and trajectories of the church; he was committed to preaching and leading worship as an expression of *logos*, of Christ-in-the-world; he was willing to stand up against the principalities and powers; he was willing to love the non-Christian neighbor as a fundamental religious practice. Lesser-known aspects of Bonhoeffer include his support of Christian unity and his work as a youth minister.

As a pastor, he traveled as a global citizen and remained an *inhabitant of the church*. Yet his church became more broadly defined as the world itself as an acknowledgement of the failure of Christendom, leading to an ecclesiological shift grounded in Jesus' enduring question: "Who do you say that I am?" (Matthew 16:13, Mark 8:27, Luke 9:18). Bonhoeffer writes:

> What keeps gnawing at me is the question, what is Christianity, or who is Christ actually for us today? The age when we could tell people that with words—whether with theological or with pious words—is past, as is the age of inwardness and of conscience, and that means the age of religion altogether. We are approaching a completely religionless age; people as they are now simply cannot be religious anymore. Even those who honestly describe themselves as "religious" aren't really practicing that at all; they presumably mean something quite different by "religious."
>
> ....
>
> What does a church, a congregation, a sermon, a liturgy, a Christian life, mean in a religionless world? How do we talk about God—without religion, that is, without the temporally

conditioned presuppositions of metaphysics, the inner life, and so on? How do we speak (or perhaps we can no longer even "speak" the way we used to) in a "worldly" way about "God?" How do we go about being ἐκ-κλεσία [*church, literally, those who are called out*], those who are called out, without understanding ourselves religiously as privileged, but instead seeing ourselves as belonging wholly to the world?[2]

But if Bonhoeffer believed that Jesus has "left the building" of the church, where does this leave the pastor as an inhabitant of the church?

Implicated.

The Patron Saint of Deicide

Any pedestrian reading of Bonhoeffer's works beyond a few cherry-picked essays here and there will expose that ecclesiology (that is, *the theology of the church*) is absolutely essential to his theology. Given his relationship with the church and state at the end of his life, his writings about the church are far more cataclysmic when the whole of his life and work is considered. While the church had abandoned him long before he found himself in prison, his commitment to the *logos* of the Christ is the thread strung throughout his writings, and this thread is stronger than any human failure to destroy "the church." The church of his time had, he believed, failed, but Bonhoeffer's Christology planted the seeds for an experimental ecclesiology which prioritized Christ as the hope of the world and the church the necessary and proper platform

---

[2] Bonhoeffer, *Letters and Papers from Prison* (30. April 1944), *DBWE* 363-345, in Green and DeJonge (eds.), 777-778.

for Christ to be known and made known. Even when preaching is bad, Bonhoeffer maintained in earlier work, the *logos* is present in proclamation and the celebration of sacrament because of the necessary connection between Christ and His Body, that is, the church.

Clearly the church has failed Christ, and not just on the level of local, institutional failure, but systemic, cultural, international failure. In this recognition of failure, we should listen also for the devastation and disappointment of German Idealism latent in Bonhoeffer's writings which (like his contemporary, Paul Tillich) seems to echo Nietzsche's approach to Idealism. The belief in a coming new era of peace is central to Christian affirmations of Second Coming; however, this peace without taking the complexities and intersectional reality of Christ as both historical figure and as present human reality is a phony and cheap peace. The church as a whole is implicated as complacent in this ongoing charade and devaluation of Christ. Karl Barth's influence on Bonhoeffer is perhaps most clearly seen on this point, but Bonhoeffer's acceptance of the reality of genocide and connecting the obvious link between evil and the institutional church is his point of departure from Barth.

For this reason, I recognize Dietrich Bonhoeffer as perhaps the first truly radical theologian in the 20th century who emerged from Euro-American Christianity. His legacy has yet to be truly and fully actualized as a radical Christian pastor. For those of us who have chosen (and are called) to remain in the implicated church Bonhoeffer's challenge is posed to us to reclaim the radicalism of the Christian message; the iconoclasm of Christian hope; and the harsh reality of recognizing, naming, and untangling the racism, sexism, homophobia, and xenophobia within the church.

These fears and hatreds are gods which can and should be killed in any continuing authentic Christian theology. The church—whatever we might mean by "the church"—must be the stomping ground of this graveyard of gods. Could we then name Bonhoeffer the patron saint of deicide?

Bonhoeffer's challenge is total, and it is one which few could live faithfully. Which is why a stronger, tamer, white-washed Bonhoeffer has been systemic and intentional. It is safer to render him only a martyr for what is rendered to be a "true," "pure"—*white*—American evangelical Protestantism. As the story goes, the Americans arrived just a few weeks too late to the Flossenbürg Concentration Camp, just over two miles from the Czech border. The mythology has posited American Christianity to have nearly been the savior of one of the saviors of the faith.

The Confessing Church

This little liturgy is meant to offer *something* for the semisesquicentennial of Bonhoeffer's martyrdom. It is primarily a confession and reflection for clergy but if all believers are indeed priests, it is for everyone. Please use it on your own, please modify it for your theological persuasion. My own use of it will probably be in private or in conjunction with a few like-minded pastoral colleagues.

The spirit of the Chrism Mass is invoked by the fact that the seventy-fifth anniversary is also Maundy Thursday in this year of writing, 2020. Maundy Thursday is often when Catholics celebrate Chrism Mass, but the liturgical date invokes betrayal and human failure. I am reminded of Søren Kierkegaard's later writings, describing the church as making a fool out of God. Maundy Thursday is a day we remember that Jesus' first disciples betrayed God,

Godself. And they betrayed God out of financial interest, out of safety, out of fear, and out of a longing to return home.

And we know the story: Jesus was mocked and made to be a fool. The fear of the disciples (Mark 16:8), however, is not the last word, and foolishness is indeed one of the ways by which we may consider our adherence to Jesus (or at least Paul says so, in 1 Corinthians 4:10).

Indeed, we have much to confess.

I make these assumptions in this liturgy. The church stands in need of confession, and clergy must be honest about our history, tradition, and failure. The church is made of imperfect persons, of course, but systemic evil is demonic. My intended confession is that that I make a mockery of God in my own believed fidelity to God, and embodying this foolishness is one of the ways I aspire to conform to the shape of the one I proclaim to be present in bread and wine. The liturgy is a confession of the clergy for our own infidelity and the church's complacency. I hope to have conversations about this liturgy with my colleagues and friends about how we can live out the doctrine of the priesthood of all believers in new and relevant ways, and how we who continue the church after the martyrdom of Bonhoeffer—and with him, the death of Christendom—in like manner aspire the church to be a *confessing* church.

Schema

This short work is part of my larger pastoral and scholarly project of developing radical Christian theology in the church. I have previously published two books of sermons which employ radical theology for preaching, *Too Good to*

Be True and *The World is Crucifixion*. With Natalie and Jesse Turri we have created three devotional coloring books—*Coloring Advent, Coloring Lent,* and *Coloring Women of the Bible*—based upon radical theology.

My first academic book, however, was *The Synaptic Gospel,* which explored the intersections of affect neuroscience and religious experience, specifically how worship itself can be a form of religious education when worshipers develop empathy for one another. In the book I matter-of-factly invoke one of Friedrich Nietzsche's questions posed by his character of the madman:

> What festivals of atonement, what sacred games shall we have to invent?[3]

In our secular and secularizing culture, where religion is not disappearing but changing into something new, ritual remains a human necessity, to mark time and space, especially in times of uncertainty—and especially in eras of birthing of new gods in America (as Neil Gaiman so forcefully presents in his novel, *American Gods*).[4] *The Bonhoeffer Chrism Mass* is a contribution to this question.

Acknowledgements

This is the inaugural publication of Barber's Son Press, and I thank the reader for purchasing this book to support my own theological and pastoral calling. Thank you, also, to those who offered reflections to be included in this book. Barber's Son Press is named for my father, who tirelessly cut hair for decades to support our family.

---

[3] Friedrich Nietzsche, *The Gay Science*, trans. W. Kaufmann (New York: Vintage, 1974), §125.
[4] Neil Gaiman, *American Gods* (New York: W. Morrow, 2001).

Briefly: I wish to recognize Dr. John Aupperle, a United Methoist pastor and professor at Saint Vincent College, who introduced me to Dietrich Bonhoeffer in a college course innocently titled "Protestant Traditions."

And my congregation, St. Paul's United Church of Christ in Dallastown, Pennsylvania, which is the site of my continued learnings, both humbling and hopeful, who walk with me on my own spiritual journey.

Finally, my Bonhoeffer seminar students at Lexington Theological Seminary have pushed me to go deeper with Bonhoeffer and have underscored the exigency of Bonhoeffer to the church.

Thank you.

Christopher D. Rodkey
Epiphany, 2020

INTRODUCTION TO

THE CHRISM MASS

The Chrism Mass is celebrated in traditional forms of Western Christianity, typically during Holy Week and often on Maundy Thursday. The mass is a celebration of ordained ministry and the sacramental appointment of the pastorate or priesthood and often involves a renewal of vows of ordination. The mass also serves a function of exhibiting episcopal authority, by the bishop then distributing the special oils to be used in priestly functions throughout the coming year, transferred by a special rite called the Rite of the Reception of Oils.

Pope Paul VI (1897-1978) specifically re-instituted the practice of the Chrism Mass in its modern form based upon an ancient version for which evidence exists into the second century. His decree of re-institution explains that "The Chrism Mass is one of the principal expressions of the fullness of the bishop's priesthood and signifies the closeness of the priests with him." Furthermore:

> In order to strengthen (priests') spiritual life and the sense of priesthood, it is most desirable that... every priest... renew the act by which he committed himself to Christ and by which he promised to carry out the priesthood's responsibilities, especially to observe celibacy and obedience to his bishop.... Also, that in this spirit he celebrate the gift, sealed by the sacrament of orders, that is his calling to service of the Church.[1]

---

[1] Archbishop Edwin O'Brien, "Chrism Mass a Privileged Moment," *Catholic Review* (19. January 2012), online.

The most ancient form of the Chrism Mass was some sort of consecration of oils used for the priestly duties during the Easter Vigil or Holy Saturday.

That is, in the *absence* of God in the world, in that moment of the salvation of the world while Christ stands in Hell, the gifts of the priestly office are consecrated to bring about the hope, healing, love, and justice which Christ empowers the church through the Holy Spirit.

The pushing out of God in the world is a significant theme in Bonhoeffer's later writings. This theme, along with a corporate confession of the pastor and the church as a whole, is the centerpiece of this liturgy.

Instructions and Preparations

I offer this liturgy with the hope and expectation that it will be experimented, modified, challenged, and changed. The liturgy may be used by individuals in solitary settings or with small groups of clergy who remain accountable to each other. While the Chrism Mass is primarily written with clergy speaking their confessions of the church, it is not strictly bound to being exclusive for clergy to use.[2]

This liturgy requires some preparation. First, it requires some sort of oils for anointing, perhaps oils important to your own religious traditions. Ideally, there are two

---

[2] I define "clergy," too, quite broadly as anyone engaged in ministry, clearly recognizing that in my own and other traditions organization is neither the litmus test nor the identifier for ministerial calling and preparation in many contexts. In fact, the use of this liturgy by laity to claim as an act of the priesthood of all believers is one of the ways the Chrism Mass may be employed.

different kinds of oils—one for everyone and another for clergy—they could be the same.

Second, performing the Chrism Mass requires some planning around the "Offering," a part of the liturgy when individuals or groups will offer their reflections, hopes, plans, dreams, and visions to each other.

I envision the Offering a kind of "free-form confession" but it is one specific to those who are authorized ministers in one way or another. The instructions found there in the liturgy are based upon Bonhoeffer's proposed book outline, which he offers in one of his last letters. Bonhoeffer's proposal was no less than a reassessment and re-evaluation of Christianity. The book's conclusion was to be directed toward clergy and how the church of the future should be led:

> Conclusions: The church is church only when it is there for others. As a first step it must give away all of its property to those in need. The clergy must live solely on the freewill offerings of the congregations and perhaps be engaged in some secular vocation. The church must participate in the worldly tasks of life in the community—not dominating but helping and serving. It must tell people in every calling what a life with Christ is, what it means "to be there for others." In particular, *our* church will have to confront the vices of hubris, the worship of power, envy, and illusionism as the roots of all evil. It will have to speak of moderation, authenticity, trust, faithfulness, steadfastness, patience, discipline, humility, modesty, contentment. It will have to see that it does not underestimate the significance of the human "example"…; the church's word gains weight and power not through concepts but by

example…. Further: revision of the question of "confession" (Apostolikum) [*Apostle's Creed*]; revision of apologetics; revision of the preparation for and practice of ministry.[3]

In this part of the liturgy I pose the following questions or topics for clergy or leaders to discuss with one another.

In the coming year, what property is my church giving away, and to whom?

How will my church newly serve those in this community and "be there for others?" Who specifically will receive this service?

How will my church and my leadership exhibit and embody a spirit of humility and debasement of power in service to its mission?

How will my congregation witness against the vices of hubris, the worship of power and envy, and voices which present things that are false to be true?

and

How will my ministry and personal actions demonstrate exemplary witness against the vices of hubris, the worship of power and envy, and voices which present things that are false to be true?

How will my congregation witness to moderation, authenticity, trust, faithfulness, steadfastness, patience, discipline, humility, modesty, contentment?

---

[3] Bonhoeffer, *Letters and Papers from Prison* (3. August 1944), *DBWE* 503-504, in Green and DeJonge (eds.), 814-815.

and

How will my ministry and my lifestyle be an exemplar of moderation, authenticity, trust, faithfulness, steadfastness, patience, discipline, humility, modesty, contentment?

How will I newly preach and teach the orthodox tenets of the Christian faith? How will I challenge orthodoxies in the efforts to "be there for others" and be Christ for this community?

How will I seek new ways to defend the Christian faith? How will I live to make my defense empirically and visibly true?

How will I newly engage or approach religious education for younger people? How will I speak of vocation with younger people?

How will I newly engage and contribute to theological or vocational education? How will I support others in their preparation to enter ministry?

How can I be a good steward of any compensation I receive from my congregation?

How am I working toward or engaged in a secular vocation?

How will I offer confessions in the coming year? Who will keep me accountable?

Each statement should be concluded with the words "The church is church only when it is there for others."

Confessio

The primary idea behind this Chrism Mass is a reversal of its Roman Catholic manifestation. Where the "traditional" (though thoroughly modern) rendering is an act of authority of the episcopacy over the priests—and simultaneously, preservation and policing of the successive hierarchy of the church—this Chrism Mass is the representative of the church being held accountable to God.

Liturgies commemorating martyrdom traditionally invoke many names of the martyrs, and this liturgy names Bonhoeffer not so much a "saint" in the canonical sense, but a pastoral exemplar of Christ and part of our Cloud of Witnesses in the present day. Those litanies often end or penultimately praise:

> Lamb of God, who takest away the sins of the world,
>
> *Spare us, O Lord.*
>
> Lamb of God, who takest away the sins of the world,
>
> *Graciously hear us, O Lord.*
>
> Lamb of God, who takest away the sins of the world,
>
> *Have mercy on us.*

Addenda

The reflections presented at the end of this book are offered simply as examples of reflections which could be offered or used to begin the process of priming and shaping the confession at the centerpiece of the Chrism Mass. They are all provocative in different ways, and may even be offensive to some. If the latter is the case, direct energies toward what Tillich called the "theology of offense." Offer *your* contribution about how *you* move offensively, that is, forward.

Finally, the appendices present other martyrs celebrated on April 9, possible scripture readings for use in the Chrism Mass, and a conspectus of how and when April 9 will occur upon the Western liturgical calendar in the coming years.

THE CHRISM MASS

OPENING

Jesus Christ did not come to this world to condemn it, but in order to save it.

> *We have relied upon the Mark of Cain as our hope, rather than the saving power of Jesus.*

And to Jesus, the weakness of God, may we ascribe all glory and power.

Amen.

THE SOLEMN DECLARATION

O burning Mountain, O chosen Sun,

> O perfect Moon, O fathomless Well,

O unattainable Height, O Clearness beyond measure,

> O Wisdom without end, O Mercy without limit,

O Strength beyond resistance, O Crown beyond all majesty:

> The humblest thing you created sings your praise.[4]

A trinitarian or some other opening statement may be added here, if meaningful or desired.

---

[4] Mechtilf of Magdeburg, as quoted from Don Saliers, "Aesthetics," in *The Wiley Blackwell Companion to Christian Mysticism,* ed. J. Lamm (Hoboken, NJ: Wiley Blackwell, 2017), 84.

THE CONFESSION

From a multiplicity of callings and contexts, O God,

> *We assemble to pronounce our guilt*
> *and to proclaim our hope.*

As we reflect upon the calling of the priesthood of all believers,

> *We give pause, and give thanks,*

But recognize that the Christ is bigger than all of us.

The first things will pass away,

> And tears will be wiped from eyes,

But we have failed to approach the hurt, the pain,

> *The systemic evil,*

> *The racism, the classism, the sexism,*

> *Which we in the church have throughout history perpetuated.*

We have not loved the stranger.

We have not loved the teenager.

We have not loved the pastorate.

We have not loved the laity.

We have not loved the lost or the lonely.

We have not stopped for the half-dead child of God

    laying on the side of the road.

We have approached the earth with scapegoating

    instead of stewardship.

Silence.

We have neglected the immigrant,

We have exaggerated our courage,

We have chosen the easy route.

We have abandoned the student.

We have exploited the seminarian.

We have shunned the risk-takers.

We have blamed the young.

We have forgotten the old.

We have worshiped Empire.

We have lifted colonial power above the cross.

We have lusted after power which is not from the weakness of God.

Silence.

We have lied about our support of the Jew and Muslim.

We have tamed the horror of genocide

       as a distant history

Without truly recognizing that the *Shoah*

       continues, and the blood is on our hands.

Silence.

We have lied that the afterlife is a meritocracy

       gained by our lips and imaginations alone.

We have insulted God by equating the divine with capital,

       and thereby worshiped Satan in the Church of Jesus.

Silence.

We come gathered to confess our sin.

We sabotage our ability to deeply gaze into mirrors.

We call upon the Christ who is the Word Made Flesh,

 imploring to be with us in the Church.

For we must prepare for the arrival of the Christ

 into this body which has abandoned him.

Prepare the way with oil and thanksgiving,

 with wine, and corn, and wheat,

 and sacrifices which come from the heart,

 and tears of pain transfigured into tears of joy.

Silence.

O God, this Church which you have gifted to us

 which is the true throne of Christ

 needs to be stripped,

needs to be made bare,

laid open and exposed,

to give birth and new life to this world,

    to us as individuals,

    to us all as priests,

    to us all as children seeking parental reconciliation.

Silence.

Today we name the cost of discipleship—

knowing that words are never enough.

Today we name martyrs who have truly paid the price.

Here martyrs may be named, such as Dietrich Bonhoeffer, Martin Luther King, Jr., Edith Stein (St. Teresa Benedicta of the Cross), or others whose memories and witness you wish to invoke.

Today we untangle the Mark of Cain that has poisoned your Church,

and soaked in your cup of blessing,

and baked into your loaf which has suffered for us.

Today we confess in hope of bodily transfiguration—

> to necromance this Church,

> to whet these bones,

> to call upon the collision of heaven and earth—

> and for the grace to have bold enough voice and witness to call upon these miracles.

Silence.

Today we call upon the resurrection from the graves:

> so we may rejoice in a multiplicity of one Spirit,

> and we may go from this place to enact the healing,

> and speak in tongues of fire, Pentecosting—

> until we all see with our own eyes end to neither dawning nor sunset

> and we rejoice in the shade of the leaves of healing.

Silence.

And we call upon Christ

>whom we invoke, invite, and provoke,

>praying that he is found at home again

>in the church that is his body and future kingdom,

>the church that is his power,

>>imperfect, humbling, and weak,

>the church that is his glory of humility and overcoming,

>forever, becoming, without end—

>*Amen.*

SCRIPTURE

Here scripture readings may be read. Several suggestions are offered in Appendix I.

OFFERINGS OF REVISION AND REVERSAL

See instructions found in this liturgy's introduction. Following each statement or each speaker, repeat the corporate phrase:

> *The church is church*
>
> *only when it is there for others.*[5]

MEDITATION ON THE PRIESTHOOD[6]

Who am I?

Who do you say that I am?

Who do others say that I am?

Am I really what others say of me?

Or am I only what I know of myself?

Like a caged bird striking the walls of its cage,

>   longing for freedom,

>   starving for colors, for flowers, for music,

>   thirsting for kind words,

---

[5] Bonhoeffer, *Letters and Papers from Prison* (3. August 1944), *DBWE* 503, in Green and DeJonge (eds.), 814.

[6] Adapted from Dietrich Bonhoeffer's poem in *Letters and Papers from Prison* (21. August 1944), *DBWE* 459-460, in *The Bonhoeffer Reader*, ed. C. Green and M. DeJonge (Minneapolis, Fortress, 2013), 816-817.

desiring human intimacy,

shaking with rage at power, lust, and pettiest insult,

passively awaiting something better, or for my savior to arrive?

Am I worried about things I cannot control?

Too tired and empty to pray?

Too exhausted to think?

Too busy to work? *Really* work?

Weary, and lusting for death as an easy way out?

Who am I?

Am I this one, or am I the other one?

This one today, and tomorrow another?

Am I both simultaneously?

Am I appearing before others a hypocrite?

Am I appearing to myself as a victim?

Or is what remains in me like a defeated army,

freeing in disarray from a victory that is already won?

Who am I?

Who do you say that I am?

Who do others say that I am?

Am I really what others say of me?

Or am I only what I know of myself?

These lonely questions mock me.

Whoever I am, you know me.

And God, *I am yours.*

COMMUNION

If appropriate, with others, the Eucharist may be celebrated at this time.

RITE OF CONSECRATING THE CHRISM

A reading from the Hebrew Bible, the Torah:

"I call Heaven and Earth to witness against you today:

> I place before you life and death,
>
> Blessing and Curse.

Choose life so that you and your children will live.

> And love God, your God,

listening obediently… firmly embracing…

affirming: God is life itself!

Life itself is poured out onto the soil

Entrusted to our ancestors."[7]

Blood and soil!

Blood and soil!

From the earth the voice of your siblings' blood petitions for mercy!

Blood and soil! *Blood and soil!*

From the graves of the idolaters of privileged living space!

From the dirt dusting the engraved golden plates!

Is this soil fertile or barren?[8]

Is this soil promised to our ancestors?[9]

Blood and soil! *Blood and soil!*

But stones wear smooth.[10]

And soil erodes.

---

[7] Based upon Deuteronomy 30:19-20 (MSG).
[8] Numbers 13:17-20.
[9] Deuteronomy 11:18-21.
[10] Job 14:18-22.

God made the soil, just as God made the sky.[11]

But God kissed the ground,

     and breathed life into the dirt,

and from the mud arose the first human!

God exhaled human life as gift,

Do we ever exhale as God?

Do we give life with breath?

Does our exhaust entrust hope undeservedly?

Has God ever stopped exhaling?

The fountain of blood arises, calling out from the soil

     at the true birth of humanity.

Blood and soil!

God exhales life into the soil,

     but we inhale death.

The exhaling of God—the *ruach*—

     the anointing,

---

[11] Psalm 146:3-9.

the pure essence of breath

arises humanity, mud and exhaustion.

This is our anointing, this is our chrism,

breath and mud.

Like the seeds on good soil, breath gives life.

THE PRAYER OF FAITH

Are any among you suffering?[12]

Let us pray.

Are any among you sick?

Let us call for the elders to pray over us with oil.

In prayer the Lord will raise you. Your sins will be forgiven.

> *So we confess to one another, and pray for one another, for the healing of all of God's people.*

If we wander away from You, we are called to be brought back;

when we return, we are forgiven;

when we lead others to return, we represent Christ for others.

---

[12] James 5.

Our prayer of faith is that God's word be fulfilled,

> not of our own doing, but of our own celebration,

> and that our actions provoke the coming of Christ.

Amen.

ANOINTING OF
THE PRIESTHOOD OF ALL BELIEVERS

You, my friends, are a chosen people.[13]

You are a holy nation of royal priests.

As such, you reflect the goodness of God,

> *who has called us out of darkness, and into the light.*

We are all followers of a single priest, Jesus,

> and all followers of Jesus are priests in his Name.

No one should regard us as anything

but ministers of Christ

> and dispensers of the mysteries of God.[14]

You are worthy, as the Lamb is worthy

> rewarded in the wealth and wisdom of God

---

[13] 1 Peter 2.
[14] Martin Luther, in the prelude of *The Babylonian Captivity of the Church*; 1 Corinthians 4.

in its slaughter.

To the one seated on the throne, and to the Lamb

    be blessing, honor, glory, and might

       forever and ever!

Amen!

    Amen!

Amen!

    Amen![15]

All believers, laity and clergy alike, may elect to be anointed with oil.

ANOINTING OR SEALING FOR
THE ORDAINED OR AUTHORIZED CLERGY

To those who are called to keep the sheep:[16]

You are beautiful, you are worthy.

You are called to speak with tongues of fire.

You are called to minister with tenderness and mercy.

You are called to sing healing to the hurt.

---

[15] Revelation 5.
[16] 1 Samuel 16.

You have found favor in God's sight.

Relieve others and be relieved.

Clergy or other ministers may be anointed with chrism or oil, preferably administered by a layperson.

AGNUS DEI[17]

Lamb of God, who takest away the sins of the world,

    Spare us, O Lord.

Lamb of God, who takest away the sins of the world,

    Graciously hear us, O Lord.

Lamb of God, who takest away the sins of the world,

    Have mercy on us.

HYMN

A hymn, poem, or other reading may be included.

DISMISSAL

All believers: keep this Gospel, and live it.

Do not seal words of prophesy with wax or oil,

---

[17] Traditional, after John 1:29 and 36.

but let them flow, for the time in near.

The Sprit and the bride of Christ say,

> *"Come."*

May everyone who hears the Word

> and encounter it with us say,

> *"Come."*

Let everyone who is thirsty,

> *come.*

Let anyone who wishes to drink from the water of life

> *take it as a gift from God.*

Do not turn on your calling.

Do not silence your prophesy.

Be assured, for Jesus lures us, saying,

> "Surely, I am coming soon."

Amen.

> *Come, Lord Jesus!*

May the grace of the Lord Jesus be with all the saints.
                              Amen.[18]

---

[18] Revelation 21.

REFLECTIONS

A Disciple's Prayer

John Bair

O Lord my God:

may our actions spring from our responsibility to You, and
not from our own thoughts;

may we act

> in obedience to You,
> rather than in preaching to others;

may we follow

> Your example,
> and leave a better world for future generations;

may we live

> for You in faith,
> and not seek to prove Your existence to others; and

may Your words be music, and a fountain of joy,

> that purifies our character in times of sorrow.

Help us, Lord,

> to view others not by what they do,
> but instead by what they suffer;

help us

> to endure any suffering in allegiance to You,

and not view the cross as tragedy;

help us

      to avoid cheap grace and to live in repentance,
      discipleship, and the grace of the cross;

help us

      to have a faith, that our spirit can use as a weapon,
      in the struggle against our flesh;

help us

      to deny ourselves and see only You,
      the One leading us, on the road before us; and

help us

      to be stewards of Your word
      for those who have asked to hear and understand it.

Thank You, Lord,

      for judging us in love,
      saving us from the judgement of envy and hatred;

thank You

      for illuminating our evil,
      and showing us how all are entitled to grace; and

thank You

      for providing the courage to sinners,
      and the victims of sin, to do Your will.

Lord, whatever our lives may bring, Thy name be praised.

Amen.

on a cross like a body on a tree

Carla Christopher

martin
luther used
as a sharpened stake
through hearts
beneath a yellow star
the cross
a handle

we hang our hopes like a body
on a cross like a body on a tree

so much we place
upon
our heroes
asking them to
redeem us

When I Remember Bonhoeffer, I Feel Like a Fool

John B. Cobb, Jr.

I think of myself as a serious Christian in the sense of one who seeks sincerely to be a disciple of Jesus.

The story of Bonhoeffer makes me wonder how serious I am.

Under what circumstances would I be willing to give my life?

I live in a world governed by institutions and individuals who repeatedly make commitments and announce policies more destructive to our planet and its inhabitants than those of Hitler.

I sometimes complain, but never in such a way as to effectively end the mad rush to self-destruction.

Since I complain more than most, I sometimes feel self-righteous.

When I remember Bonhoeffer, I feel like a fool for this self-congratulation.

He did not end the rule of evil either.

But, like Jesus, he took actions that were commensurate with the evil he opposed.

Like Jesus, Bonhoeffer tried.

Are there any circumstances in which I might really try?

God Calls,

God Bids Us Come and Die

John C. Dorhauer

Dietrich Bonhoeffer is a spirit still moving in the body of Christ today. While in Germany recently, I met with hundreds of pastors—many of whom are reminded of his words and message to them. Everywhere I travel now throughout the United States, I find clergy reading again his letters, sermons, and books.

He serves still as a call to the ordained that when God calls, God bids us come and die—reminding us that our vow to serve the Gospel is always greater than our allegiance to earthly powers.

I carry his spirit with me everywhere I go. In a time when forces align to do harm to others in the name of the risen Jesus, his words and actions stand as an example of courage in the struggle for peace and justice.

He reminds me that any power or privilege I have I must use to speak truth to power, to stand against any resistance to Christ's love, and to demonstrate over and over again that the body of Christ was built to heal the world, not oppress it.

Losing May Be

the Only Win Possible

Jon Ivan Gill

The witness of Bonhoeffer inspires me toward a secular theology of meaningful commitment in the midst of speculative dissonance.

While I might always reside in the space between chaos and order, Bonhoeffer—from his short residence in New York at Union to his encounters with the Nazi regime and eventual death—represents a Kierkegaardian leap into the fight for justice, even when justice isn't readily justifiable for my own well-being.

At the cusp of a humanistic theology that divinizes the human and can go in several directions, Bonhoeffer lures me into a wager on the people and contexts at/of the margins, knowing full well at the outset that losing may be the only win possible.

God Did Not Choose

Jeff Hood

Though the Evangelical Movement has often been unable to ascertain the difference between their collective ass and a hole in the ground, they have courageously refused to cede the crucifixion to the demythologizing fantasies of their secular enemies.

For that we should all be most grateful.

Because the cross is where we come face to face with what it means to be human... and even more... what it means to be divine.

Golgotha is not an attractive destination... but surely it is the destination of all those who choose to believe in the transcendence of divinity or the transcendence of love.

I hate the church. By "church," I mean that huge evangelical church across the street. When I see those dumbass slogans in flashing lights, I just want to blow my breakfast all over myself.

I hate that shit.

But try as I might, I can't ignore them.

Not too long ago, I noticed the cross on top of the church. The crucifixion drew me in.

In that moment, I heard the voice of my creator: *"Would you die for them?"*

Immediately, my mind went to the glorious martyrdom of Dietrich Bonhoeffer.

But then, I started thinking about the less glorious scenario of dying for a bunch of cheese dicks at the local evangelical church.

With that, I turned up the damn radio as loud as I could. For that, I repent.

Bonhoeffer wrote that "when Christ calls someone, he bids him come and die"... that "the cross is laid on every Christian."

God didn't get to choose who he was going to die for.

God... just *died.*

The Evangelical Movement has constantly reminded me that the crucifixion is an invitation to follow God...an invitation to die... no matter what.

Forgive us for living beyond that... them... Amen.

Pushed out of the World

Josh de Keijzer

Bonhoeffer died.

And then he rose again.

"Resurrection?" —in the words of theologians, students, and believers, all having stared into the abyss of his martyrdom wondering what might have come of this man and his theology had he lived. They engaged his ethics, his theology, his resistance, his thoughts about Christianity in a secular age. They made meaning. Thus Bonhoeffer, in accordance with the richly-layered complexity of his thought and the unfinished business of a life cut short before its time, became what people wanted him to be: the conservative, the radical, the progressive, the philosopher, the liberal.

Relatively few, however, have made the effort to understand Bonhoeffer on his own terms by digging into his academic writings, difficult, nerdy, arrogantly intellectual as they are.

Yet it is there that one finds the key to his theology and, in a way, the reason why he died.

Bonhoeffer's theology in *Sanctorum Communio* and *Act and Being* ought to be read as a theology of the cross deeply influenced by Luther's theology. Particularly in *Act and Being*, Bonhoeffer sought to articulate a theological method that (against Barth), through a synthesis of idealism and realism, sought to validate theological claims by means of a hermeneutical praxis borrowed from Heidegger.

His self-involving "method" leads to a discovery of the reality of God's self-revelation in Christ through participation of believers in and with Christ.

The only knowledge of Christ is found in living out Christ in the world as community. Christ cannot be mastered cognitively and objectively but only seen and understood subjectively and concretely in the enactment of what Christ calls us to be.

Bonhoeffer dug the grave of his intellectual pride. Little did he envisage the ultimate consequences of such a praxis.

If in *Act and Being* this praxis describes the church predominantly for itself and its own life, where the church is Christ existing as community, Bonhoeffer's later works problematize this being. Through his work in Barcelona and his encounter with the black church in Harlem, Bonhoeffer came to understand how Christ manifests as—and in—the marginalized and suffering. His disappointment in the German Christian movement gradually reinforced this displacement of divine presence. Together with his increasing emphasis on the world and its embodied reality, this disappointment led to an ambiguous assessment of God's presence in the world.

As he languished in prison, he began to understand that the divine presence—given *in* and *with* Christ—he wrote so eloquently about in his academic period was being pushed out of the world. He realized that this was part of who God is but also that this expulsion was particularly acute in the modern world: God is present precisely in the absence demanded by a world come of age.

We live before God as if there is no God. The praxis of Christ leads to the marginalization and eventually the extermination of Christ. Thus comes the inevitable consequence of the radical proposal of Bonhoeffer's theology that links revelation with self-involving praxis: Bonhoeffer himself is pushed out of this world.

Bonhoeffer dies. And we stare into the mystery of a life lived under the cross, trying to make meaning, wondering if such a praxis is worth the price.

We May End up at The Gallows

Kristina I. Lizardy-Hajbi

In the midst of scorching nationalism that burned hatred into hearts and bodies to ash, Bonhoeffer's life and witness remain as one of the better-known examples of active resistance and outright dissent in World War II's Nazi Germany.

What do his words and actions say about our own resistance tactics to the tyrannies that the United States government inflicts upon the world's bodies *en masse?*

What should our response be to children who die at our borders, or unarmed black teenagers killed at the hands of law enforcement, or trans women brutally murdered for living in beauty and love? How should we respond when the political whims of our mad dictator and his Gestapo lead to the senseless murders of Kurds, or Syrians, or Palestinians, or refugees and asylum seekers the world over?

The faith of Bonhoeffer is our faith, should we accept its radical gospel message.

Let us "share in the trials of this time with [our] people"* by publicly blasting, undercutting, and destroying the evils both within and beyond a church that is often in collusion with power and destruction.

We may end up at the gallows, but we may save our humanity.

---

* Eberhard Bethge, *Dietrich Bonhoeffer: Eine Biographie* (Munich: Christian Kaiser Verlag, 1967), 736.

What Will Lead us out onto The Street?

Jordan E. Miller

We must learn to live in the world as if there were no God. There is no God who will save us. We are our own need-fulfillers and problem-solvers. The responsibility is ours alone.

The charge comes from both directions.

Politically, we are responsible for fulfilling our own needs and solving our own problems.

Theologically, we are challenged to affirm God's absence from our religious experience. Dietrich Bonhoeffer once wrote that "[Hu]man[ity] is summoned to share in God's sufferings at the hands of a godless world."*

If God is to be found, it is in suffering and absence—our experiences of a lack of God. Reflecting on Bonhoeffer, William Hamilton also wrote, "In order to overcome the death of the father in our lives, the death of God, the mother must be abolished and we must give our devotion to the *polis*, to the city, politics, and our neighbor."†

Radical theology is and must be political theology. We are called to forsake God to love humanity. Communion becomes possible only without God. And a theology of God's absence is and must be a political theology. God's absence will lead us out onto the street.

---

* Dietrich Bonhoeffer, *Letters and Papers from Prison*, ed. E. Bethge (New York: Touchstone, 1997), 361.
† Thomas J. J. Altizer and William Hamilton, *Radical Theology and the Death of God* (Indianapolis: Bobbs-Merrill Company, 1966), 44.

The Patron Saint
of Preachers Who Suck

Christopher D. Rodkey

As a preacher I weekly struggle with the double-bind of American Christianity in the early 21st century: I must communicate the Gospel, but I cannot alienate my audience. I have been told so many times that my preaching sucks that twice in my short career I swore off preaching and took steps to bar myself from the pulpit. As it happens, going to graduate school was one of my escape plans from preaching every Sunday.

I think nearly every preacher can relate. I've had people tell me I was lying about the scripture and stormed out never to see them again. I've had someone threaten to cut my salary for preaching against war. Not too long ago a family walked out—never to be seen again—saying that I was being discriminatory while preaching a sermon decidedly against discrimination. Surely, those who wish to discriminate felt left out. I obsessed over that for weeks.

One time I even had someone tell me that as a Christian they felt that Jesus was too liberal, too radical, and that's not what they want to hear on Sundays. Fair point. My pews are barely occupied, and people vote with their feet.

I rely too much on notes, I don't tell enough jokes, I carry myself like an elitist, I'm full of myself, I don't talk enough about my children, I'm unrelatable, I'm too serious, I talk too fast, I talk too slow. I talked about money a few times. I'm too honest. I used a Pennsylvania Dutch word and this is an English-speaking church. I talk too much about the Bible.

These things may or may not be true, but it's exhausting and regularly humiliating. I often feel like my margin of error is so slim in preaching that I have to obsess about choosing the right words, trying not to offend, but still embrace an offensive gospel.

These are the sins and aspirations of the 21st century preaching.

Bonhoeffer is a saint to me in many ways but one of them is as a saint for those whose preaching sucks.

Surely one of the Gods whose Satan I worship is one which paints myself as a hero and exemplar of faith, one worthy of standing in a pulpit on a weekly basis (see, for example, Bonhoeffer's *"Sicut Deus"* in *Creation and Fall*). Also emphatically undeniable is that this calling, lure, and command to preach the Gospel is not uniquely a calling of the ordained. It is a kind of atheism to believe that preaching is conditional upon myself being the one who speaks.

Bonhoeffer's writings are Good News to the one whose preaching sucks. The Word proclaimed is the Word, even if it's boring, even if its presentation is ineffective.

The Word must be proclaimed by everyone, even if their preaching sucks. The more preaching sucks, the more it must be preached.

If the Gospel is one of God being pushed out of the world, so also should one's preaching proclaim the God pushed out of the world and our call to follow. Standing in the pulpit, I often feel as if I have a responsibility not to push God out of the world for my audience, afraid they will give up on faith, or simply say "I'm done," or "I am no longer a Christian."

To wit: preaching that sucks *can* and *ought* to push out from the world all those within earshot and empower them to in like manner lead others out of this world to seek God.

Sometimes that might push the preacher out of the pulpit.

Sometimes we need to be pushed out from the pulpit.

APPENDIX I

SUGGESTED SCRIPTURE READINGS
FOR THE CHRISM MASS

The following suggestions are offered for scripture readings for the Chrism Mass. All of the following are from the New Revised Standard Version (NRSV) of the Bible.

Option #1:
Traditional Readings
for the Roman Chrism Mass

Isaiah 61:1-9

The spirit of the Lord GOD is upon me,
    because the LORD has anointed me;
he has sent me to bring good news to the oppressed,
    to bind up the brokenhearted,
to proclaim liberty to the captives,
    and release to the prisoners;
to proclaim the year of the LORD's favor,
    and the day of vengeance of our God;
    to comfort all who mourn;
to provide for those who mourn in Zion—
    to give them a garland instead of ashes,
the oil of gladness instead of mourning,
    the mantle of praise instead of a faint spirit.

They will be called oaks of righteousness,
    the planting of the LORD, to display his glory.
but you shall be called priests of the LORD,
    you shall be named ministers of our God;
you shall enjoy the wealth of the nations,

and in their riches you shall glory.

Because their shame was double,
  and dishonor was proclaimed as their lot,
therefore they shall possess a double portion;
  everlasting joy shall be theirs.

For I the LORD love justice,
  I hate robbery and wrongdoing;
I will faithfully give them their recompense,
  and I will make an everlasting covenant with them.

Their descendants shall be known among the nations,
  and their offspring among the peoples;
all who see them shall acknowledge
  that they are a people whom the LORD has blessed.

Psalm 89:21-22, 25, 27

[M]y hand shall always remain with him;
  my arm also shall strengthen him.
The enemy shall not outwit him,
  the wicked shall not humble him.

I will set his hand on the sea
  and his right hand on the rivers.

I will make him the firstborn,
  the highest of the kings of the earth.

Revelation 1:5-8

(Grace to you and peace from him who is and who was and who is to come, and from the seven spirits who are before his throne... [Rev. 1:4b])

[A]nd from Jesus Christ, the faithful witness, the firstborn of the dead, and the ruler of the kings of the earth.

To him who loves us and freed us from our sins by his blood, and made us to be a kingdom, priests serving his God and Father, to him be glory and dominion forever and ever. Amen.

Look! He is coming with the clouds;
    every eye will see him,
even those who pierced him;
    and on his account all the tribes of the earth will wail.
So it is to be. Amen.

"I am the Alpha and the Omega," says the Lord God, who is and who was and who is to come, the Almighty.

Isaiah 61:1 (leading to Gospel)

The spirit of the Lord GOD is upon me,
    because the LORD has anointed me;
he has sent me to bring good news to the oppressed,
    to bind up the brokenhearted,
to proclaim liberty to the captives,
    and release to the prisoners;

Luke 4:16-21

When he came to Nazareth, where he had been brought up, he went to the synagogue on the sabbath day, as was his custom. He stood up to read, and the scroll of the prophet Isaiah was given to him. He unrolled the scroll and found the place where it was written:

"The Spirit of the Lord is upon me,
   because he has anointed me
      to bring good news to the poor.
He has sent me to proclaim release to the captives
   and recovery of sight to the blind,
      to let the oppressed go free,
to proclaim the year of the Lord's favor."

And he rolled up the scroll, gave it back to the attendant, and sat down. The eyes of all in the synagogue were fixed on him. Then he began to say to them, "Today this scripture has been fulfilled in your hearing."

Option #2
Readings Concerning Martyrdom

Philippians 4:11-14

Not that I am referring to being in need; for I have learned to be content with whatever I have. I know what it is to have little, and I know what it is to have plenty. In any and all circumstances I have learned the secret of being well-fed and of going hungry, of having plenty and of being in need. I can do all things through him who strengthens me. In any case, it was kind of you to share my distress.

1 Peter 4:14-16

If you are reviled for the name of Christ, you are blessed, because the spirit of glory, which is the Spirit of God, is resting on you. But let none of you suffer as a murderer, a thief, a criminal, or even as a mischief maker. Yet if any of you suffers as a Christian, do not consider it a disgrace, but glorify God because you bear this name.

Matthew 5:10-12

"Blessed are those who are persecuted for righteousness' sake, for theirs is the kingdom of heaven.
"Blessed are you when people revile you and persecute you and utter all kinds of evil against you falsely on my account. Rejoice and be glad, for your reward is great in heaven, for in the same way they persecuted the prophets who were before you.

Revelation 6:9-11

When he opened the fifth seal, I saw under the altar the souls of those who had been slaughtered for the word of God and for the testimony they had given; they cried out with a loud voice, "Sovereign Lord, holy and true, how long will it be before you judge and avenge our blood on the inhabitants of the earth?" They were each given a white robe and told to rest a little longer, until the number would be complete both of their fellow servants and of their brothers and sisters, who were soon to be killed as they themselves had been killed.

Option #3
Readings Offered in Commemoration
of the Ministry of Dietrich Bonhoeffer

Hebrews 13:5-7

Keep your lives free from the love of money, and be content with what you have; for he has said, "I will never leave you or forsake you." So we can say with confidence,

"The Lord is my helper;
  I will not be afraid.
What can anyone do to me?"

Remember your leaders, those who spoke the word of God to you; consider the outcome of their way of life, and imitate their faith.

Philippians 3:10-17

I want to know Christ and the power of his resurrection and the sharing of his sufferings by becoming like him in his death, if somehow I may attain the resurrection from the dead.

Not that I have already obtained this or have already reached the goal; but I press on to make it my own, because Christ Jesus has made me his own. Beloved, I do not consider that I have made it my own; but this one thing I do: forgetting what lies behind and straining forward to what lies ahead, I press on toward the goal for the prize of the heavenly call of God in Christ Jesus. Let those of us then who are mature be of the same mind; and if you think differently about anything, this too God will reveal to you. Only let us hold fast to what we have attained.

Brothers and sisters, join in imitating me, and observe those who live according to the example you have in us.

Romans 12:1-8

I appeal to you therefore, brothers and sisters, by the mercies of God, to present your bodies as a living sacrifice, holy and acceptable to God, which is your spiritual worship. Do not be conformed to this world, but be transformed by the renewing of your minds, so that you may discern what is the will of God—what is good and acceptable and perfect.

For by the grace given to me I say to everyone among you not to think of yourself more highly than you ought to think, but to think with sober judgment, each according to the measure of faith that God has assigned. For as in one body we have many members, and not all the members have the same function, so we, who are many, are one body in Christ, and individually we are members one of another. We have gifts that differ according to the grace given to us: prophecy, in proportion to faith; ministry, in ministering; the teacher, in teaching; the exhorter, in exhortation; the giver, in generosity; the leader, in diligence; the compassionate, in cheerfulness.

Matthew 16:24-26

Then Jesus told his disciples, "If any want to become my followers, let them deny themselves and take up their cross and follow me. For those who want to save their life will lose it, and those who lose their life for my sake will find it. For what will it profit them if they gain the whole world but forfeit their life? Or what will they give in return for their life?

APPENDIX II

A BONHOEFFER CALENDARIUM

A few Christian sects—most significantly Lutheran and Anglican—identify Dietrich Bonhoeffer as a saint or as a modern-day martyr. The following is a list of saints, martyrs, and others who are our Cloud of Witnesses venerated on April 9 or who died on April 9, many of which are martyrs who may be significant to the reader.

Abdiesus (+362 AD) was a one of the the **Holy Martyrs of Persia**, executed by King Sapor II of Iran.

St. Acacius of Amida (+425 AD) was a Mesopotamian Bishop (in modern-day Turkey) whose compassion for those in poverty became famous and inspired many. He sold all of his furnishings with value within his churches to alleviate the suffering in his community.

He was also famous for prompting reconciliation and peace. Word of his generosity spread into the Neo-Persian Empire, prompting Emperor Bahram V to seek Acacius' presence. Legend maintains that Acacius' compassionate spirit so inspired the Emperor that the meeting halted hostility between the Sassanid and Byzantine Empires.

St. Agamund (+870 AD); see **the Martyrs of Croyland**.

Mikael Agricola (+1557 AD) was a major figure in the Protestant Reformation in Finland. His prayer book, along with his translation of the New Testament into Finnish, set the foundations of what is today understood as the Finnish language. He died while returning home from negotiating the peace agreement which ended the Russo-

Swedish War. Some Lutherans celebrate his life like a saint on April 10, but he died on April 9.

St. Askega (+870 AD); see **the Martyrs of Croyland**.

Francis Bacon (+1626 AD) is one of the primary firgues associated with philosophical empiricism. He was a devout Anglican Christian and argued forcefully for the integration of Christianity and science.

St. Bademus and his disciples, of Persia (+376 AD): St. Bademus was an Abbot and martyr who was executed with several other Christians for refusing to convert to Zoroastrianism. He is also called St. Bademe and St. Vadim; some recognize his feast day on April 10.

Basil of Lesbos (+1463? AD) is one of **the New Martyrs** in the Orthodox tradition and is the father of **St. Irene of Lesbos**. See **the New Martyrs**.

St. Casilda of Toledo (+c. 1050 AD), daughter of Yahya ibn Ismail al-Mamun, King of the Muslim taifa of Toledo in the 11th century, who offered compassionate and merciful care to Christians who were imprisoned. She later converted to Christianity following an illness and spent the rest of her century-long life of asceticism in Burgos, in modern-day Spain.

St. Castorius (+287? AD); see **the Martyrs of Pannonia**.

St. Claudius (+287? AD); see **the Martyrs of Pannonia**.

Bl. Demetrio da Tifliz (+1321 AD) is one of the **Martyrs of Thane**, in modern-day India. As a layman he had likely been a missionary to China and India. He was arrested and executed with **St. Thomas of Tolentino** and **Bl. James of Padua**.

St. Demetrius of Thessalonica (+305? AD), also called "Demetrius of Sermimum," is traditionally rendered as a "military saint," that is, a saint often venerated by soldiers. The son of a family known for their piety, Demetrius was impaled in Thessalonica (in modern-day Greece) during a persecution attributed to the Roman Emperor Galerius.

The Feast of St. Demetrius is also celebrated by many Christians on October 26, and still others on November 8.

St. Eleni of Lesbos (+1463? AD), also venerated as **Susanna**, is one of **the New Martyrs** in the Orthodox tradition, and is said to be the cousin of **St. Irene's** cousin. See **the New Martyrs.**

Hieromartyr Desan (+362 AD) was a Bishop among the **Holy Martyrs of Persia**, executed by King Sapor II of Iran.

St. Donatus (+303/304? AD), one of the **Martyrs of Sirmium.**

St. Dotto (+6ᵗʰ cen.AD) founded a monastery in the Scottish Orkney Islands, which is said to be a place of healing.

St. Egdred (+870 AD); see **the Martyrs of Croyland**.

St. Elfgete (+870 AD); see **the Martyrs of Croyland**.

St. Eupsychius of Caesarea in Cappadocia (+4ᵗʰ cen. AD), believed to have been the son of a Senator, was arrested and tortured for his faith, but then released. While in prison, legend holds that an angel healed him.

When he was released from the prison, he gave away all of his belongings—including to those who persecuted him. A second arrest was ordered by the Roman Emperor, Julian the Apostate, and Eupsychius was harshly tortured and beheaded.

St. Fortunatus (+303/304? AD), one of the **Martyrs of Sirmium.**

The Four Crowned Martyrs (+287? AD) or **Quattro Coronati** include the **Martyrs of Pannonia**, whose Feast Day is jointly recognized by some as April 9. See **the Martyrs of Pannonia.**

The Four Martyrs of Thane (+1321 AD) are **St. Thomas of Tolentino, Bl. James of Padua, Demetrio da Tifliz,** and **Peter of Siena.** They were executed in Thane, in modern-day India, for blasphemy against Islam. They are celebrated together with a Feast Day on April 9, but only Thomas is officially or traditionally recorded as a Saint independent from the others.

St. Gaucherius (+1140 AD) at a young age became a hermit and attracted followers while a teenager. He later founded a monastery in France.

St. Grimkeld (+870 AD); see **the Martyrs of Croyland.**

St. Hedda (+870 AD) was a Benedictine Abbot who was murdered with eighty-four other monks off of the coast of England by pagan Danes as one of **the Martyrs of Croyland.** Centuries later St. Hedda's gravestone would become a pilgrimage site.

Raúl Silva Henríquez (+1999 AD), a Salesian monk and Archbishop of Santiago de Chile, he was a political and religious activist called "a constant thorn in the government's side."

St. Hugh of Rouen (+730 AD) was an exceptional Benedictine Abbot and later Bishop in France, who retired into a simple lifestyle of a monk until the end of his life.

St. Irene of Lesbos (+1463? AD) is one of **the New Martyrs** in the Orthodox tradition. Her parents Basil and Maria brought her with them to warn monks on the island of Lesbos of invading Turks. When the Turks arrived they killed the monks and then turned to Irene's family, whose father was a well-known mayor.

Irene was tortured in front of her parents, dismembered and then suffocated, and then Basil and Maria were executed. Today Irene is fondly venerated as a virgin martyr and her remains were uncovered with evidence of her torture in 1961. See **the New Martyrs.**

Bl. James of Padua (+1321 AD) is one of the **Martyrs of Thane**, in modern-day India. A Franciscan, he had likely been a missionary to China and India. He was arrested and executed with **St. Thomas of Tolentino** and **Bl. Demetrio da Tifliz.**

C. E. M. Joad (+1953) was a well-known English philosopher, television commentator, pacifist, and environmental activist. Late in life he publicly converted to Christianity.

William Law (+1761 AD) was a major Anglican theologian, mystic, and literary figure, who was massively influential on generations of English intellectuals, including **John Wesley.** He is celebrated with a Feast Day by many Anglicans on April 10, but he died on April 9.

St. Marcellus of Die (+463 AD), a French Bishop who was exiled from Gaul for his defense of the Christian faith.

Maria of Lesbos (+1463? AD) is one of **the New Martyrs** in the Orthodox tradition and is the mother of **St. Irene of Lesbos**. See **the New Martyrs**.

Maribus (+362 AD) was a Presbyter among the **Holy Martyrs of Persia**, executed by King Sapor II of Iran.

The Martyrs of Croyland (+870 AD) were Benedictine monks under the leadership of their Abbot, **St. Hedda**. They were murdered by pagan Danes along the coast of England. Among the eighty-four killed are **Sts. Agamund, Askega, Egdred, Elfgete, Grimkeld, Sabinus, Swethin, Theodore,** and **Ulrich**. They are all commemorated on the same Feast Day, April 9.

The Martyrs of North-West Africa (+459 AD), also known as **the Martyrs of Regiis, the Martyrs of Aquae Regiae,** and **the Martyrs of Arbal**, were the victims of a massacre of Christians during the Easter Mass of 459 in Algiers. Those who were not killed by ambush during the worship service were later tortured and executed, and the invading Vandals desecrated the sacramental elements following the killings.

The Martyrs of Pannonia (+287? AD) are considered to be five of the nine early Christian Saints called the **Four Crowned Martyrs** or **Quattro Coronati** and some have different Feast Days in varying traditions.

Legend holds that the Martyrs of Pannonia were artists ordered by the Roman Emperor Diocletian to create a sculpture of the Roman god Asclepius to be used as an idol for a temple. The four were trapped into coffins and then throne into the Sava River. Traditionally, though unverified, their names are remembered as **Sts. Claudius, Castorius, Symphorian, Nicostratus,** and **Simplicus.**

The Martyrs of Persia (+362 AD) or **Holy Martyrs of Persia** were executed by King Sapor II of Iran. Among them were 270 martyred plus **Bishop Desan, Presbyter Mariabus,** and **Abdiesus. St. Ia** was one of the martyrs, she is commemorated individually on September 11.

The Martyrs of Sirmium (+303/304?) are comprised of two groups of saints all killed in what is modern-day Kosovo. The first were roughly seventy killed together for their Christian faith. Tradition holds that among the first group may have been **Sts. Fortunatus** and **Donatus.** The second group were seven virgins who were martyred separate from the others. Some celebrate their Feast Day separately on February 23.

Associated with the Martyrs of Sirmium is one of the most important saints, **St. Anastasia the Pharmakolytria** ("deliverer of portions"). She is liturgically known as one of the "Great Martyrs" and in some traditions the afternoon Mass on Christmas Day is celebrated in her remembrance; her Feast Day is December 25.

St. Materiana (+6th cen. AD), is also known as **Mertheriana, Merthiana, Madrun,** or **Madryn**; *"merthyr"* is Welsh for "martyr." Daughter of King (and Saint) Vortimer, her legend describes a young oman of privilege and royalty whose life was largely spent on the run from wars ensuing around her.

The Commemoration of the Translation of the Relics of St. Monica of Hippo (+387 AD), also known as **Monica of Tagaste**. St. Monica is best known as the faithful mother of **St. Augustine of Hippo**, and her Feast Day is celebrated on August 27 by some Christians and on

May 4 by others. Her remains were moved at least three times after her first burial. When the relics were moved from the second site in Ostia (southwest of Rome) to Rome, miracles are were reported to occur along the way or during the "transition." Her remains are now in the Basilica of Sant' Agostino, Rome, built in honor of her son.

The New Martyrs (+1463? AD), also known as **the Newly Revealed Martyrs**, are Orthodox **Saints Raphael, Nicholas, Irene**, and **Eleni of Lesbos.** Their remains were miraculously uncovered in 1960. Several others were killed together, including St. Irene's parents, Basil and Maria, her young cousin Eleni (who is also venerated as Susanna), and a local teacher named Theodore. After their remains were uncovered locals claimed to have witnessed the martyrs.

St. Nicholas of Lesbos (+1463? AD) is one of **the New Martyrs** in the Orthodox tradition. He was captured by Turks on the island of Lesbos and was forced to watch **St. Raphael** be tortured and killed before his own execution. See **the New Martyrs.**

St. Nicostratus (+287? AD); see **the Martyrs of Pannonia.**

Bl. Peter of Siena (+1321 AD) is one of the **Martyrs of Thane**, in modern-day India. A Franciscan, he had likely been a missionary to China and India. Following the arrest and execution of **St. Thomas of Tolentino, Bl. James of Padua,** and **Bl. Demetrio da Tifliz**, Bl. Peter was arrested and executed a few days later. He is memorialized together with the others as the Martyrs of Thane on April 9.

The **Quattro Coronati** or the **Four Crowned Martyrs** (+287? AD) include the **Martyrs of Pannonia**, whose

Feast Day is jointly recognized by some as April 9. See **the Martyrs of Pannonia.**

St. Raphael of Lesbos (+1463? AD) is one of **the New Martyrs** in the Orthodox tradition. He spent much of his adult life as a priest and monk on the run from invading Turks, and he was arrested and violently executed in 1463. See **the New Martyrs.**

St. Sabinus (+870 AD); see **the Martyrs of Croyland.**

St. Simplicus (+287? AD); see **the Martyrs of Pannonia.**

St. Swethin (+870 AD); see **the Martyrs of Croyland.**

St. Symphorian or **Simpronian** (+287? AD); see **the Martyrs of Pannonia.**

St. Theodore (+870 AD); see **the Martyrs of Croyland.**

St. Thomas of Tolentino (+1321 AD) is one of the **Martyrs of Thane.** A Franciscan, he had likely been a missionary to China and India. He was arrested with two other Martyrs of Thane, tortured, and executed, and the fourth martyr, **Bl. Peter of Siena**, was beheaded a few days later.

They were executed in Thane, in modern-day India, for blasphemy against Islam.

St. Ulrich (+870 AD); see **the Martyrs of Croyland.**

St. Waldetrudis (+688 AD), also known as **Waudru** and **Waltrude**, was the wife of **St. Vincent Madelgarus.** Vincent joined a monastery in 642 and Waldetrudis followed suit to begin a convent in the Hainaut province of

Belgium. Together they were the parents of **Sts. Dentilin, Landericus, Madalberta**, and **Adeltrudis**.

Christian Wolff (+1754 AD) was an iconoclastic German philosopher who argued for religious tolerance and proposed new metaphysics for understanding God and reason.

*

Other inspiring individuals who died on April 9:

Andrea Dworkin (d. 2005), Jewish feminist philosopher and anti-war activist who forcefully argued against the exploitation of women in her landmark philosophical work on pornography.

Egon Bondy (d. 2007) was a Czech philosopher and literary figure who is best known as part of the "Prague Underground."

Dorrit Hoffleit (d. 2007) was a noted American astronomer who inspired generations of young women to pursue scientific inquiry.

Rabbi Joseph Soloveitchik (d. 1993), called "the Rav," deeply influential American philosopher best known for his opposition to Adolf Hitler.

Tsien Tsuen-hsuin, better known as **T. H. Tsien** (d. 2015), Chinese scholar who preserved and advanced the study and understanding of Chinese literature.

Frank Lloyd Wright (d. 1867), a lifelong Unitarian, is today one of the most important and influential American architects.

APPENDIX III

A BONHOEFFER CONSPECTUS

A schedule of when April 9 appears on the calendar for several following years.

April 9, 2020	Maundy Thursday
April 9, 2021	Friday; day immediately following Yom HaShoah
April 9, 2022	Saturday before Palm Sunday
April 9, 2023	Easter Sunday
April 9, 2024	Season of Eastertide
April 9, 2025	Season of Lent
April 9, 2026	Maundy Thursday (Eastern calendar)
April 9, 2027	Season of Eastertide
April 9, 2028	Palm Sunday
April 9, 2029	Season of Eastertide
April 9, 2030	Season of Lent
April 9, 2031	Holy and Great Tuesday (Holy Week)

April 9, 2032	Friday; day immediately following Yom HaShoah
April 9, 2033	Saturday before Palm Sunday
April 9, 2034	Easter Sunday

AUTHOR

Christopher D. Rodkey is Pastor of St. Paul's United Church of Christ in Dallastown, Pennsylvania, and teaches itinerantly at Penn State's York campus and online for Lexington Theological Seminary.

also by Christopher D. Rodkey

The Synaptic Gospel: Teaching the Brain to Worship. University Press of America, 2010.

Too Good to Be True: Radical Christian Preaching, Year A. Christian Alternative, 2012.

The World is Crucifixion: Radical Christian Preaching, Year C. Noesis, 2014.

Coloring Lent, with Jesse Turri and Natalie Turri. Chalice, 2017.

Coloring Advent, with Jesse Turri and Natalie Turri. Chalice, 2017.

Coloring Women of the Bible, with Natalie Turri. Chalice, 2018.

Dreaming in Color: A Reflection Guide for Coloring Women of the Bible. Chalice, 2018.

The Palgrave Handbook of Radical Theology, edited with Jordan Miller. Palgrave Macmillan, 2018.

CONTRIBUTORS

John Bair is a seminary student studying philosophy and theology, currently enrolled at Lexington Theological Seminary.

Carla Christopher is a Lutheran pastor, poet-activist, and former Poet Laureate of York, Pennsylvania. She currently divides her time between work as a regional cultural competency trainer and is working as a certified redevelopment pastor at a congregation in Lancaster, Pennsylvania.

John B. Cobb, Jr., is one of the United States' leading theologians, most prominently known for his advancement of process philosophy within mainline Christian circles. His many books include *Is it Too Late?* and co-author of *For the Common Good* and *Process Theology: An Introductory Exposition.*

John C. Dorhauer serves currently as the 9th General Minster and President of the United Church of Christ. He completed his doctoral studies in white privilege and is the author of two books, *Steeplejacking: How the Christian Right is Hijacking Mainstream Religion* and *Beyond Resistance: The Institutional Church Meets the Postmodern World.*

John Ivan Gill teaches philosophy, religious studies, theology, and English at Pomona College; California State University, Dominguez Hills; Norco College; and Claremont School of Theology. He has written multiple articles on Afrofuturism, religion, hip-hop, philosophy, post-structuralism, atheism, and creative writing. As a rapper and hip-hop musician performing under the name Gilead7, he is part of the rap collective Tomorrow Kings and co-owner of Serious Cartoons Records and Tapes in

San Bernardino, California. His most recent book is *Underground Rap as Religion: A Theopoetic Examination of a Process Aesthetic Religion*.

Jeff Hood is a nationally-known Baptist preacher, author, and activist. His books include *The Courage to be Queer* and *The Executed God*.

Josh de Keijzer is a theologian, communications consultant, and author of *Bonhoeffer's Theology of the Cross*.

Kristina Lizardy-Hajbi is the Director of the Office of Professional Formation and Term Professor of Leadership and Formation at Iliff School of Theology, Denver, Colorado.

Jordan E. Miller is an independent scholar and community organizer from Newport, Rhode Island. He is the author of *Resisting Theology, Furious Hope: Secular Political Theology and Social Movements* and co-editor of *The Palgrave Handbook of Radical Theology*.

Barber's Son Press

York, Pennsylvania

www.ingramcontent.com/pod-product-compliance
Lightning Source LLC
Chambersburg PA
CBHW031223090426
42740CB00007B/685